PIPPA WALLER

FLOW

The Essential Guide to Living an Optimal Life, Learn Valuable Information and Useful Advice That Can Help You Towards Optimal Living

Descrierea CIP a Bibliotecii Naţionale a României
PIPPA WALLER
    FLOW. The Essential Guide to Living an Optimal Life,
Learn Valuable Information and Useful Advice That Can Help
You Towards Optimal Living / Pippa Waller – Bucharest: Editura
My Ebook, 2020
    ISBN

PIPPA WALLER

F L O W

The Essential Guide to Living an Optimal Life, Learn Valuable Information and Useful Advice That Can Help You Towards Optimal Living

My Ebook Publishing House
Bucharest, 2020

TABLE OF CONTENTS

CHAPTER 1

THE BASICS ON LIVING AN OPTIMAL LIFE

Synopsis

"Don't you ever get the feeling that all your life is going by and you're not taking advantage of it? Do you realize you've lived nearly half the time you have to live already?" - Ernest Hemingway, The Sun Also Rises

Are you living your life to the fullest? For some people, living an optimal life is like wishing to win the lottery. Others consider it as a daunting or overwhelming task that requires time, effort, and money. However, contrary to what these people believe, living life to the fullest is easier to achieve with few changes in their lifestyle, perception, and views.

The Basics

In just simple ways, you can already live a saner, more satisfying, and healthier life without sacrificing your responsibilities at work, to your family, and at home. Whether you are living in the city or in a small town, you can make a change and live an optimal life. How?

➤ *Learn to Appreciate Even Little Things*

Instead of your usual grabbing a cup of coffee, driving to work, and returning home after a whole day of stress, why not break this typical daily routine and learn to appreciate the things around you. Listen to the different sounds that nature produces and be aware of the beautiful surroundings that you often overlook due to the overwhelming responsibilities that you have.

➢ *Be the Real You*

Some individuals choose to hide the real them with the fear that their friends or colleagues will not accept them for who they are. However, making positive changes in life starts by loving and accepting yourself and being proud of who you are. Stop judging yourself as this put limit to the things that you can do and achieve. It is true that there are a certain part of the society that may not accept you, but what important is that you are courage to be yourself. Do what makes you happy and the ones that you're good at because life is what you make it.

➢ *Be Happy and Adventurous*

This may sound simple, but being happy is always a choice. You can choose to either end all your sufferings and give yourself the time to enjoy life or remain miserable until you can no longer deal with it.

Part of being happy is to do things that can give you some excitement and adrenaline rush such as the ones you fill when you accomplish something you never dream of doing. Engaging in adventures and embracing new challenges will make your life more exciting.

➤ *Find Your Purpose and Don't Give Up*

Every individual has his own purpose in life. Finding something to live for and knowing your life meaning will enable you to become motivated to live a better and more fulfilling life. You have to clearly set your goals and determine what you want to achieve. This way you can easily identify the things that you have to take in order to achieve such goals. Along the path, you may experience life challenges that may test your courage, determination, and faith. The best thing that you can do is to be strong enough and committed to doing the best that you can overcome these trials no matter how big they are. Not accepting defeat and being motivated to reach your goals help you manage simple and even complicated things in life, and eventually achieve optimal living.

➤ *Listen to What Your Heart Says and Connect With Soul*

When in doubt about something, following your instinct seems to be the best option. You can ask for opinions or recommendations from the people you trust but in the end, you have the final say. You have to be confident when making important decisions in your life because of all people, you are the one who knows the things that are good for your and those that will have a negative effect in your life and the people around you.

Connecting with and rejuvenating with your soul makes it easier for you to focus more on what makes you happy, contented, and peaceful. Regardless of your spiritual beliefs, everything that you do in your life will have a significant impact on the lives of others. In this case, why not strive to make a positive change in this world and inspire more people to become better individuals?

The Key Components of Living an Optimal Life

In some cases, due to a series of unfortunate events and certain circumstances, living a fulfilling and meaningful life can become a daunting task. Basically, you need to have a healthy physically emotionally, spiritually, and psychologically in order to live an optimal life. However, balancing these aspects is truly not that easy. Improving certain areas of your life can be an excellent way to make your journey less difficult.

✓ **Practice Healthy Living**

The modern society has different perceptions about individuals with unhealthy lifestyle or scruffy appearance. More opportunities for growth and personal improvement as well as greater chances for optimal living will be yours if you practice healthy living. This may include having a healthy and active lifestyle and healthy relationship with the people around you.

✓ Strive to Learn Continually

Great things in life can be achieved if you are not afraid to make mistake and improve yourself by learning new things. Having the interest to enhance your knowledge and improve your skills will inspire and motivate you to become innovative and creative when making life changes and choices.

✓ Find Emotional and Spiritual Peace

Living an optimal life cannot be fully realized if you failed to deal with your emotions and recognize the value of spirituality. You are the only one who can control your emotions. For this reason, it is vital that you

have a clear idea and understanding of the factors that affect your emotional state. This way, you will know how to manage these factors in order to achieve emotional peace, which is crucial in achieving great happiness. Aside from this, emotional peace can also be achieved by learning to forgive. On the other hand, spiritual peace will make you aware of the oneness of life and acknowledge the things that will significantly improve your life and the world as a whole.

CHAPTER 2

IDENTIFY WHERE YOUR LIFE HAS ISSUES

Synopsis

As mentioned, your chances of living an optimal life depend on how you manage the different aspects of your life. In this regard, it is important that you identify the areas of your life that have issues. By determining your areas of concern, it will already be easy for you to look for possible solutions to such issues. They areas may include:

Where Do You Have Issues

Social Relationships

Life is best enjoyed with presence of those who are dearest to you (i.e. family, friends, partner etc.) However, not having a good relationship with these people will have a great impact on the quality of your life. Improving your relationship with your loved ones is not as difficult as it seems. Most of the time, respect, honesty, trust, time, care, and support are what you need to become socially acceptable regardless of who you are.

Health Condition

The best joy in life can be experienced by being healthy and doing all the things that you love to do with the people you love in a perfect environment. Your general health will pay a significant role in all your plans and the decisions that you have to make in your life. Poor physical health can be a hindrance in your plans to participate in various physical activities and even in performing your day-to-day tasks.

Emotional Problems

Like social relationship, different negative emotions and perceptions affect your goal of living an optimal life in more ways than one. These types of emotions include the feeling of inferiority, embarrassment, guilt, and inadequacy as well as stress, irritability, and sadness.

Career

Having a regular job and earning enough money to pay for your needs and luxuries are not enough to experience optimal living. You should love what you are doing. If your job is just causing you stress yet you choose to stick to it because it pays better, then you will not completely experience the joy that life has to offer. Experts advised that those who are unhappy with their current job should pursue something that they are passionate about.

Having a job that is related to your interests allows you to purse your real passion.

CHAPTER 3

IDENTIFY IF YOU ARE CAUSING ISSUES

Synopsis

You have dealt with the factors that prevent you from experiencing optimal living. How come you are not still living a quality and contented life? There are two parts of life that you have to balance and manage efficiently for you to live an optimal life: Yourself and External Influences.ş

Identify Issues

Most of the time, determining and managing the issues that influence you life will not be enough as you also need to resolve the issues in your personal life. Self-defeating behavior and pessimism contribute to personal problems. If you are unwilling to make changes due to fear of failure, they you have failed even before trying.

Keeping your personal issues under control increases you chances of achieving personal and professional success as well as living an optimal life. The quality of your life can be determined by your thoughts. This means that if you believe that your life sucks, then it will really suck. Having the right mindset will keep you motivated to live your best life.

Sick and tired of your usual routine? This is because doing the same things over and over again can make you feel impatient and stagnant. Stagnancy in life is a sign of deeper issues that need to be resolved. Oftentimes, you feel stagnant because there is nothing that excites you to take action. Trying something new and making new experiences can make your life more interesting.

Living an optimal life starts with your own self. You have to be ready to take new challenges, try new things, and make changes. Accepting your faults and learning from your mistakes allows you to move forward.

CHAPTER 4

WHAT DO SEE AS AN OPTIMAL LIFE

Synopsis

"Somebody should tell us, right at the start of our lives, that we are dying. Then we might live life to the limit, every minute of every day. Do it! I say. Whatever you want to do, do it now! There are only so many tomorrows."

- Pope Paul VI

Every individual has his own view of how he will live an optimal life. Regardless of which path you take or what ways you choose, you can surely live the way you want to be as long as you are determined to attain it.

How Do You See It?

For some, optimal living starts by recognizing their personal responsibility. Without these, it would be easier for you to blame others for the hardships that you are suffering, be it your parents, the government, or other external entities. An optimal life is a life wherein you have the guts to accept and fulfill your responsibilities. Sure, you may experience trials that may test your faith and strength. But instead of being discouraged, why not use these hardships as an opportunity for you to grow as a person.

Optimal living means loving yourself, playing more, learning something new each day, and surrounding yourself with supportive, caring, and positive people. Living in the present, doing what your enjoy doing, and learning to forgive yourself and others also contribute to having fulfilling and worthwhile life.

Optimal life is al life with less stress, more opportunities, stronger relationship with others, and more time for yourself and your family. It can be achieved if you change your life for the better. You can start by changing how you think and perceive things. Goals and dreams in life can be realized if you make an effort to empower yourself to make successful choice and live on your own terms.

Reducing stress also serves as a key in having an optimal living. Whenever individuals feel stressed, they tend to make unhealthy choices. Physically- induced stress and emotionally-induced stress both have negative effects on your behavior.

How do you perceive an optimal life? How can you start living this kind of life? Your perception about optimal living is your key in living an optimal life. You need to understand that your beliefs have an effort on your behavior and on the actions that you have to take. In living life to the fullest, you also need to take into consideration other areas of your life that you sometimes overlook such as your education and spiritual thoughts.

CHAPTER 5

USING AFFIRMATION

Synopsis

Many individuals have negative thoughts about life especially when it comes to their job. Having this kinds of thoughts greatly influence their outlook and confidence as well as their careers, personal life, and relationships. Using positive affirmation drives positive change in your life.

Positive affirmation is defined as positive statements and thoughts that help individuals overcome negative thoughts by conditioning the subconscious mind in order for them to create a positive perception about themselves, live their best life, and develop their own reality.

Affirmations are the things that individuals say to themselves that you want to hear and believe. This serves as excellent way of starting your day. They can help change any harmful behaviors or undo that damages caused by negative thoughts. In using positive affirmation, the first thing that you have to do is to remove all the negativity in you. It would also help of you are surrounded by positive people and living in a positive environment.

How to Use Affirmation

One of the most important reminded when using affirmation is that it should be positive. This is because its main goal is to eliminate your negative perceptions about your potential, capabilities, and appearance. Counteracting these perceptions gives you the confidence to tackle and accomplish even the bigger issues. Positive affirmation has been proven to treat individuals with mental health conditions and low self esteem successfully.

Using affirmation is your first steps towards living an optimal life. Performing different affirmation exercises help you train your mind to focus more on the positive sides of life and keep you motivated. The best way to use affirmation to live an optimal life is to write them as if you have already achieved your dreams and goals.

You can write you affirmation in a sentence, paragraph, or even a whole page. It would be better if you write it short, concise, and very specific. However, you have to keep in mind that you have to believe in your written affirmations as if they were already 100% realized and true. The more you believe in whatever you are affirming, the stronger such affirmation will be.

Aside from writing your affirmations, verbally affirming your goals, ambitions, and dreams gives you a reassurance that those dreams will be turned into a reality. Using affirmation makes you believe that nothing is impossible.

CHAPTER 6

USING VISUALIZATION

Synopsis

"Everything you can imagine is real." - Pablo Picasso

Successful individuals from all walks of life are using visualization to make their life better, healthier, and happier. Visualization is considered as the best tool for achieving your goals. However, it is also one of life techniques that are often misunderstood. Not having a deeper understanding on how visualization works can result to failure.

In layman's term, creative visualization is the act of recreating sounds, feelings, and images in one's mind involving an activity to practice it a perfect environment. Unfortunately, some people failed to create a picture that is clean enough whenever they engage in creative visualization.

Visualization may seem simple, but it still requires some practice to get the best results.

Ways to Visualizes Efficiently and Clearly

Determine What You Really Want

Before you begin visualizing, you should have a clear picture of what you want to have or accomplish. Do you want to reconcile with a friend, improve your relationship with your partner, spend more time with your children, or improve your self-image?

There are individuals who think that they are not good enough. This negative perception is made worse by criticism from other people, resulting in a negative self-image. Visualization enables you to imagine yourself as someone you want to be and create a new you in your subconscious.

Creative visualization replaces your negative thoughts and beliefs with positive ones, giving you the courage to succeed in life.

Be Detail-Oriented

Details are crucial in creating a clear picture as you visualize. Using you five senses allows you to hear, feel, smell,

27

or touch your visualization. Letting go of all the tension in your body and finding a nice and quiet place where no one can bother you contributed to having a successful visualization. As much as possible, you try to hear, smell, and see everything.

Visualize Long-Term Dreams and Goals

Where you see yourself in 5, 10, and 15 years is a good subject to visualize. It would also help to visualize the personality traits that can help you attain your dreams and make your life as incredible as possible. To experience a more rewarding and satisfying results, visualize the legacies that you want to leave the word and the things that you still want to do and accomplish as a human being. Every individual has the ability to use visualization, but only few of them believe on the great contribution it has on optimal living.

CHAPTER 7

THE BENEFITS OF OPTIMAL LIVING

Synopsis

Over the past years, optimal living has provided several benefits to those who decided to accept some changes for the betterment of their lives. The social, emotional, and physical benefits that living an optimal life offers are among the main reasons why more and more individuals are clinging to this type of living.

Basically, these factors that are responsible for the happiness that you are experiencing originate with your inherent relationship and connection with the environment. As the years pass bay, individuals tend to develop rational thought processes that helps in removing pain and other negative traits, and enhances their level of happiness.

Living the best life possible and becoming that best person that you can be are the main fundamental aspects of optimal living. These aspects are interrelated with each other. The former enables you to achieve the latter, and the latter needs the former in order for it to be experienced fully.

The Factors

❖ **Optimal Living Allows You to Attain Your Goals and Be Grateful for What You Have**

A lot of people who failed to set their main goals in life often become fed-up with their lives and view the world in an unhealthy perspective. Living an optimal life involves setting up realistic and attainable goals. This gives you something to look forward to.

Achieving your dreams and overcoming the obstacles that crossed your path gives you a sense of fulfillment. However, always make it a point to be thankful for what you have. Never take for granted the people who are important to you and let your ambition rule you. Optimal living enables you to have a clearer, healthier, and better perspective towards your life.

❖ Optimal Living Encourage You to Take Chances

Seeing the world in a different perspective gives you the courage to take chances in life. This will provide excitement to your life, inspires you to educate yourself, and makes you more adventurous. The fun and joy of life can be experienced of you are living an optimal life.

❖ Optimal Living Provides You Better Health

The functional, physical, emotional, and social well-being of individuals are important elements in improving their quality of life. You will be able to manage their life properly if they have set more accessible personal goals instead of being conscious about how their health will affect their plans. Studies revealed that individuals with higher sense of well-being have better health and experience less hospitalization. Well-being makes individuals look at their health in a positive sense.

❖ Optimal Living Promotes Optimism

As mentioned in the previous chapter, pessimism prevents individuals from living life as its best. On the other hand, enjoying life to the fullest promotes optimism. Evidence suggests that optimistic people have higher quality of life than pessimists. Optimism embraces the inclination of hope and the belief that individuals can live in best of all worlds.

Additionally, being optimistic means that you view life positively. Optimists experience less stress, have increased longevity, and greater achievement than realists or pessimist. Adaptation of purpose and optimism are two variables that influence quality of life. Individuals with these characteristics adapt to stressful situations in a much better way than pessimists.

❖ Optimal Living Supports Active Living

Optimal living encourages individuals to engage in active living programs that are designed to become contributing members of the society, remain productive, and stay physically and mentally active. Individuals who participate in active living are one ones who are living their life to the fullest.

❖ Optimal Living Makes You More Responsible

Living an optimal life allows you to deal with your problems positively. Instead of sulking and letting your life waste because things did go as planned, you decide to make the necessary changes to prevent any miserable moments from happening again. You choose to live in the moment and enjoy what you have instead of becoming miserable. Optimal living eliminated all the negativity in your life.

CHAPTER 8

STAYING MOTIVATED FOR OPTIMAL LIVING

Synopsis

"Motivation is the art of getting people to do what you want them to do because they want to do it." - Dwight D. Eisenhower

Why do being motivated and staying motivated are important in living an optimal life? Success in life is possible for those who are not afraid to take actions. You work hard to achieve your targets and goals in life. Without goals, you just keep moving forward with your life without accomplishing anything.

Motivation

Self-motivation enables you to plan your goals and recognize that ways that you have to take to achieve them. It serves as a guiding force in accepting new opportunities, searching for new adventures, and trying new techniques. It gives you the willpower to improve the quality of your life and increase your level of happiness and satisfaction.

Life is a journey. There are paths that you have to take to go where you want your life to be. Along the way, you may experience boredom, tiredness, and disappointments. Motivation fuels your life and keeps you going. It prevents you from losing home even if things did not work out the way it should be. Stating motivated is the key for having an optimal life.

Living an optimal life is not the only thing that you can experience if you stay motivated. You will also avoid criticisms and earn the respect of people around you. You become more productive, inspired, and committed to feel in charge of your life.

How to Stay Motivated

You success or failure partly depends on the kind of motivation that you have. So, how will you develop motivation and stay motivated?

1. Eliminate Any Negative Thoughts

Eliminating negative thoughts and replacing them with positive ones is an excellent eat to develop and stay motivated. With just positive influences and thoughts, you will be able to think clearly and focus more on the things that need you immediate action. Most of the time, lack of faith in yourself and trust in your capabilities are what makes you think negatively.

2. Be Happy and Efficient

Doing what you love and inspires you keeps you motivated to go on with your life. The power of command and control makes you happier and more motivated to do the things that can make you live life to the fullest. Moreover, continually educating yourself and enhancing your skills gives you the assurance that you can do anything efficiently.

Being open to developments and discovering new skills helps you become more efficient, which gives you the courage to tackle all the things associated with optimal living.

3. Use Visualization

Visualization is a powerful tool for staying motivated and having optimal life. In fact, this is being used by great coaches around the world to encourage, inspire, and motivate athletes. Visualizing yourself as someone who is living an optimal life can drive you to take actions and do your best to achieve such life.

4. Remain Focused

At times, distractions may come your way, affecting your concentration. In order to keep motivated, you have to remove all the things that distract you and strive to remain focused. It is also advisable to jot down your goals so that you know what you need to work on for optimal living.

5. Seek Support

There are things in life that you cannot do on your own. Sometimes, you have to ask for the help of others especially the ones who are experts in the aspect of life that you are having difficulty dealing with. Seeking the help of someone who is successful in his chosen field and is living an optimal life will allow you to know the strategies and techniques that he used to be on the position that he is right now.

Successful people and those who benefit from optimal living are the ones who are not afraid to take actions. These actions can only be done properly if you stay motivated.

CHAPTER 9

STAYING ON TRACK

Synopsis

"Continuous effort - not strength or intelligence—is the key to unlocking our potential." - Winston Churchill

If you want to live an optimal life, then you have to know the paths you have to take, and stay on track even when life gets rough. Miserable are those who choose not to continue reaching for their dreams due to the personal issues, detours, and distractions that they may experience as they travel the path towards optimal living. Blessed are those who choose to deal with life's challenges in order to reach the road to greatness.

Staying On Track

One way to keep you stay on track is to be brave enough to deal with whatever problem that life throws at you. For instance, whenever you face detours, instead of losing hope, why not take the risk and follow this new direction. Accept the fact that they new road still have some frustrations and challenges. What is important is the fact you are able to overcome these issues, allowing you to find the right path to take.

Maintaining a healthy work and life balance also helps you stay on track. Find time to know what is right for you. This way you can live your life based on what you desire. It would also help if you create a positive relationship with the people who influence your life and the decisions that you have to make in one way or another.

Talking with someone whom you trust and with similar dilemma as yours can help you validate your feelings. There is nothing wrong with learning from the mistake of others or making them as an inspiration to living an optimal life. If you think that there is an area of your life that you cannot manage well, you should not hesitate to ask for help. You have to accept that you cannot do all things along. There will come a time that you need the help of others to get things done right.

Stress, hardships, and sorrows have become a part of life. Knowing how to manage these issues can transform you in a person who is not afraid to take the risk, grow, and live life in the best way possible.

CHAPTER 10

MAKING RESOLUTIONS FOR OPTIMAL LIVING

Synopsis

Making resolutions have become a tradition for most individuals. They typically start doing new the things included in their New Year's resolutions list at the start of the year. However, the beginning of a new year is not meant to instantly make changes in your life. This is usually the perfect time to ponder the behaviors that you have shown in the past year and make the corresponding changes to increase your changes for living optimal life.

Making resolutions for optimal living enables you to determine the things that you need to improve or change to make it easier for you to live your dream life. Unfortunately, around 88% of people make resolutions failed to stick to it.

Like other things in life, resolutions are difficult to achieve without a goal or plan to follows. As mentioned, goals allow individuals to know where they are heading. In this case, resolutions are easier to keep if you take small steps and one resolution at a time. It is also important that you stay positive and believe that you can do it no matter what.

Most people start making chance in their lives at the beginning of the year. But why start in January when you can already do it now? If you are determined to experience optimal living, you can start when you are ready.

Living an optimal life cannot be achieved in just a single month. It will take time for you to achieve you goals especially if they are worth attaining.

Patience is the key in keeping your resolutions for optimal living. It is not advisable that you accomplish all your goals in just one month. You have to give yourself the time to breathe, clear your mind, and regain the energy that you have lost as part of your efforts.

Your goals to having an optimal life can be best achieved if you divide them into smaller goals. This way, accomplishing smaller tasks on a daily basis is more feasible than trying to achieve bigger goals in the littlest time possible. Making major changes in your life that you think are impossible to achieve can

43

be made easier if you know the problems associated with it and the personal issues that you need resolved.

Your life is what you create. You can live an optimal life is you want to. You just have to be brave enough to make critical decisions, take the needed actions, and make the necessary changes. Do not let anybody put you down, you have the power to live an optimal life.

"Living your best life is your most important journey in life." - Oprah Winfrey

Printed by Libri Plureos GmbH in Hamburg, Germany